ENSURING EFFECTIVE INSTRUCTION

How do I improve teaching using multiple measures?

Vicki **PHILLIPS** | Lynn **OLSON**

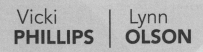

ASCD   Alexandria, VA USA

ASCD | arias™

Website: www.ascd.org   www.ascdarias.org
E-mail: books@ascd.org

Printed in the United States of America. Cover art © 2013 by ASCD. ASCD publications present a variety of viewpoints. The views expressed or implied in this book should not be interpreted as official positions of the Association.

ASCD LEARN TEACH LEAD® and ASCD ARIAS™ are trademarks owned by ASCD and may not be used without permission. All other referenced trademarks are the property of their respective owners.

PAPERBACK ISBN: 978-1-4166-1824-9   ASCD product #SF114043
Also available as an e-book (see Books in Print for the ISBNs).

Library of Congress Cataloging-in-Publication Data
Phillips, Vicki.
  Ensuring effective instruction : how do I improve teaching using multiple measures? / Vicki Phillips and Lynn Olson.
      pages cm
  Includes bibliographical references.
  ISBN 978-1-4166-1824-9 (pbk. : alk. paper) 1. Effective teaching. 2. Teachers—Rating of. 3. Teachers—Training of. 4. Lesson planning—United States. I. Olson, Lynn. II. Title.
  LB1025.3.P484 2013
  371.102—dc23
                                   2013036763

ENSURING EFFECTIVE INSTRUCTION

How do I improve teaching using multiple measures?

Want to earn a free ASCD Arias e-book?
Your opinion counts! Please take 2–3 minutes to give
us your feedback on this publication. All survey
respondents will be entered into a drawing to
win an ASCD Arias e-book.

Please visit
www.ascd.org/ariasfeedback

Thank you!

A Simple Beginning

As a teacher, how often have you reviewed a day's lesson in your head and wondered what you could do better next time? How often have you been delighted and inspired when a student suddenly grasps a difficult concept or comes up with a unique solution to a problem?

For Brittany Clark, an English teacher at Middle College High School in Memphis City Schools, every day is an opportunity for growth. When her district launched a new system for teacher development and evaluation—which included classroom observations, measures of student academic growth, and student surveys—she jumped at the chance to reflect on her practice. "I've always been really data driven," she explains, "but I'm even more so now. When I get feedback, I want to know specifics" (Bill & Melinda Gates Foundation, 2012a, p. 7).

For example, when her student survey results revealed that she could offer her students more choice among their classroom activities, she decided to give her students more options as long as they completed their original assignments. She also varied the strategies she used to check for understanding, based on feedback from her principal. In addition, she's used the same observation rubric to observe and mentor new teachers in her building. "I think it's been really beneficial in working with new teachers because it's very clear cut," she says. "I have a rubric that's really thorough. And I've started videotaping myself, so I can show new teachers. Instead of saying, 'I have a strategy that might be good,' I can just show them" (personal communication).

Teachers are vital to student learning. They want to help students succeed, and, like all professionals, they strive to keep honing their craft. Equally important, though, is the fact that most teachers want to have a say in the professional development that matters to them. Too often, unfortunately, that doesn't happen.

As recently as 2009, nearly three in four teachers didn't receive *any* specific feedback on their evaluations (Weisberg, Sexton, Mulhern, & Keeling, 2009). Imagine a football player, a concert violinist, or an airline pilot trying to improve his or her practice without the play-by-play video, audio recording, or simulation that helps each identify what went well and analyze and understand what needs improvement.

Teachers deserve to get the feedback and support that are necessary to make learning (for both their students and themselves) as powerful as possible. It's also imperative that teachers have a direct voice in shaping and improving the methods of their own evaluation and the type of professional development they receive in order to improve—both individually and collectively.

This publication addresses the questions of how teachers can collect and use strategic information to up their game and of how districts can better support teaching talent. There's been a lot written about new teacher feedback and evaluation systems, but what hasn't been discussed enough is what teachers themselves can do with this information. What we've learned as a result of our research is both encouraging and practical—ways teachers can share their practice and lessons they can learn from listening to students. The best part? Principals and teachers don't have to wait for their school systems to act before using this information to enhance their practice.

Measures of Effective Teaching

The Measures of Effective Teaching Project (MET; www.metproject.org) was a three-year research study that focused on finding multiple ways to identify effective teaching and provide teachers with actionable, reliable information they can trust to continuously improve their performance (Bill & Melinda Gates Foundation, 2013a). The project was a partnership of academics, education organizations, and nearly 3,000 teachers who voluntarily opened up their classrooms to investigate better ways to identify and develop effective teaching. This latter group included teachers in the following areas: 4th–8th grade math and English language arts, 9th grade English, algebra, and high school biology. Participating districts included Charlotte-Mecklenburg, NC; Dallas, TX; Denver, CO; Hillsborough County, FL; New York City; and Pittsburgh, PA.

What did we learn? By the end of the project, there were three primary takeaways:

1. **It is possible to identify teaching that is effective in helping students learn.** The MET study used multiple measures to evaluate teaching performance—classroom observations based on videotaped lessons, student surveys of their instructional environment, and student gains on state tests and on supplemental assessments that measured more ambitious thinking skills. During its first year, the study identified teachers who were already effective, based on these measures. In the second year, the unusual step was taken to randomly assign rosters of students to these teachers to ensure that the measures actually identified effective teachers and not just teachers with better students. The study found that teachers who were predicted to be more effective at helping students learn (based on these measures) did indeed produce greater student learning than their "less effective" colleagues. Moreover, students with effective teachers scored higher on standardized state tests as well as on other, more open-ended and challenging assessments.

2. **Multiple Measures are essential.** Teaching is complex and difficult work. It cannot be captured by a single measure—particularly a single score on a state test. The best way to evaluate teaching performance is to use a balanced approach that includes classroom observations by more than one trained observer (principals, other school administrators, or master teachers), validated student

surveys of classroom instruction, and measures of student growth on validated assessments.

3. **It's important to combine multiple measures in a balanced way when making summative judgments about teaching performance.** Otherwise, there's a risk that the other measures will be ignored and teachers will feel pressured to focus too narrowly on only one aspect of their practice. When student achievement measures are weighted between one-third and one-half of the total value, it's possible to predict which teachers will help raise students' performance.

What Your District Should Know

One of the most instructive results of the MET study is a set of nine principles for implementing high-quality teacher feedback and evaluation systems that teachers can trust. These research-based principles are also founded on the real-life experiences of teachers and administrators in Atlanta, GA; Denver, CO; Hillsborough County, FL; Memphis, TN; Pittsburgh, PA; Prince George's County, MD; Tulsa, OK; and a group of charter management organizations in Los Angeles, CA (Bill & Melinda Gates Foundation, 2013b). Since 2009, these school systems have been working collaboratively with teachers and unions to redesign how they recruit, evaluate, develop, and retain great teachers. The nine principles—grouped into three categories (see Figure 1)—are meant to help school systems implement high-quality teacher feedback and evaluation systems that are fair and reliable.

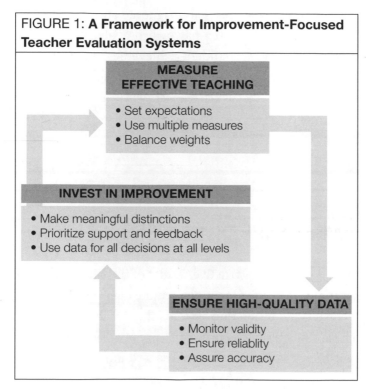

FIGURE 1: **A Framework for Improvement-Focused Teacher Evaluation Systems**

MEASURE EFFECTIVE TEACHING
- Set expectations
- Use multiple measures
- Balance weights

INVEST IN IMPROVEMENT
- Make meaningful distinctions
- Prioritize support and feedback
- Use data for all decisions at all levels

ENSURE HIGH-QUALITY DATA
- Monitor validity
- Ensure reliablity
- Assure accuracy

Category 1: Measure Effective Teaching. The first set of principles stresses that school systems should agree on a definition of high-quality practice before selecting measures that reflect those expectations. The Achievement First charter schools network, for example, has identified 24 essentials of effective instruction—grouped into 10 categories—that include "teacher uses high engagement strategies and insists on 100% students on task" and "students do most of the talking and working, teacher employs planned, rigorous questioning and pushes for top-quality oral responses and student work" (Curtis, 2011, p. 7). Teachers and school leaders within the school system need to agree on and understand the definition of effective teaching. When this is the case, appropriate expectations drive the selection of measures —and not the other way around.

Category 2: Ensure High-Quality Data. The second set of principles deals with creating information that's valid, reliable, and accurate. Like anyone else, teachers obviously don't want to expend a lot of effort trying to improve their practice if it's based on bad data. For example, it's important to make sure that student rosters accurately assign students to the right teachers. Classroom observers—whether administrators or expert teachers—need to be rigorously trained to conduct such observations, and districts need to ensure that they can observe accurately. Hillsborough County Public Schools, for example, requires observers to complete two live observation cycles to the satisfaction of a trainer. Memphis City Schools created a certification committee of teachers, principals, and administrators to establish a "gold standard" for scoring a set of teaching videos. Observers must score multiple videos within a certain range in order to ensure rater reliability.

We don't let people drive a car just because they've taken a driver's education course. We ask them to demonstrate that they can actually drive safely. By the same token, it's important to observe teachers multiple times and with multiple observers. The reasons for this are pretty simple. Teaching strategies and approaches might vary from lesson to lesson—in part based on the content for each day. Therefore, it's important to observe and make judgments on more than one lesson.

Observing a lesson using a classroom observation rubric is complex. Such rubrics include multiple competencies of teaching practice and some degree of human judgment, even though they require observers to cite evidence to support their decisions. Having more than one observer helps increase the consistency of the overall judgment. Schools and school systems can combine the number of observers and lessons watched in a variety of ways, such as by supplementing a principal's observation of a full lesson with peer observations of a different lesson.

Category 3: Invest in Improvement. The third set of principles relates to how districts and schools use teacher evaluation measures. Creating better teacher feedback and evaluation systems requires careful and painstaking work. It's a waste of time and effort to focus solely on the small percentage of individuals who require administrative action. It's critical to provide rich information to help the vast majority of teachers continually improve. That means prioritizing support and feedback for teachers. Improvement also requires using evaluation data—such as whether principals provide teachers with adequate support or whether districts provide professional development that is targeted to the areas of greatest need and discontinue programs that don't work—to inform decisions at all levels. Responsibility for improving teaching shouldn't rest with teachers alone.

Districts and schools need to be cautious about making too-fine distinctions among teachers that aren't supported by the data. Most teachers' scores on classroom observations cluster very close to the middle of the distribution. Rather than creating separate performance categories for this vast middle group that don't lead to meaningful distinctions, districts and schools would be better served to invest in helping teachers get better.

Since 2009, 36 states and the District of Columbia have made policy changes related to teacher development and evaluation (National Council on Teacher Quality, 2012). Much slower have been attempts to tie evaluation results to targeted professional development for teachers. In 2012, only 12 states required evaluations to inform professional development.

That's a big problem—and one we need to address if these new systems are truly going to help teachers continue to get better. For example, investing in innovative professional development—including the use of social networks, simulations, and remote tutors—could give teachers the help they want when they need it and put them in control of their own learning. International research provides support for the idea that high-quality teacher development systems provide systematic experiences for teachers that are self-directed, relevant, sustained, and job-embedded (Darling-Hammond, 2009). A common refrain among teachers is that so-called one-size-fits-all workshops and training seminars are outdated and ineffective methods of improving teaching practice. Districts need to give teachers more customized choices and higher-quality content, informed by data that target individual teacher's needs—including the use of video, simulations, online and blended learning courses, and teacher-to-teacher learning.

Ways for Teachers to Get Started

Teachers don't have to wait for their schools or districts to begin improving their practice today. What follows are a few ideas for how to get started tomorrow, including many that come from teachers themselves.

Self-Assess Your Practice Using an Observation Rubric

In order to improve, teachers need to be able to self-reflect upon their work. That's why self-reflection is a core component of certification by the National Board for Professional Teaching Standards and is included in many observation rubrics. Moreover, these rubrics provide a much clearer definition of high-quality practices than previous checklists and, thus, can help guide teachers' self-examination.

One way to get started is for teachers to become familiar with the competencies and domains in existing observation rubrics and think about how well they perform in each area. For example, teachers can take a look at the Framework for Teaching (www.danielsongroup.org); the Classroom Assessment Scoring System, or CLASS (http://curry.virginia.edu/research/centers/castl/class); or the Protocol for Language Arts Teaching Observations, or PLATO (http://platorubric.stanford.edu).

Teachers can discuss these rubrics to be sure they understand what's expected at different levels of performance. They can provide examples and evidence from their own classrooms that they think might meet the standards, and they can watch videos provided by the rubric developers that exemplify high-quality teaching based on the standards.

Watch Yourself Teach

Watching yourself in action is an invaluable step in the process of improving your own practice. With the technology available today (an example of which might be in your pocket or bag right now), this has never been easier.

Many teachers report that watching themselves teach— simply by viewing their own videos—is a powerful professional learning experience and changes the way they think about developing and evaluating their craft. Logistically speaking, the "how to" of recording lessons is specific to individual teachers and classrooms. Some schools choose to begin by identifying certain teachers who volunteer to record their lessons and share their practices with the entire school. By recording both veteran teachers who represent "best practices" and newer teachers who want and need coaching, the resulting exemplars cover a range of teaching styles and naturally lead to valuable discussions about the process and resulting strategies. In addition, some teachers choose to record entire class periods, whereas others try to record specific segments of particular lessons they think will be useful for sharing. Finally, it's important to carve out some time to view and respond to the videos. Many teachers watch during planning time or after school.

Katie Cardus, a middle school math teacher in the New York City Public Schools, recalls the following:

> Once the students became accustomed to the camera, the true reflective experience began. Self-reflection exercises helped me realize I needed to have more student-friendly lessons. So, instead of just teaching statistics, I used information about famous athletes. Instead of just teaching inequalities, I used signs from places around NYC and information about popular celebrities. Students then became more interested in the math surrounding this information. . . . By watching my videos and listening to the questions I was asking my students, I had the ability to revamp and improve my questioning technique. (VIVA MET Idea Exchange, 2013, p. 5)

As a result of this process, many teachers realize that they need to be a lot more reflective about their teaching on a regular basis. For example, early elementary math teacher

Kwesi Ndzibah recounts his experiences with videorecorded self-reflections:

> I was familiar with self-reflection and looking more closely at what I was teaching. But after I did my first [video] capture I was blown away. I previously would teach my math classes and not give a lot of thought to the way I was teaching. I moved from month to month, from topic to topic, until it was time for the state exams. When I saw my first capture, I really began to critique myself. *Do I really speak that fast? Why didn't I elaborate that point? I was speaking too low. Ugh, the bell rang, and I didn't get to finish this concept, or I don't like the way that lesson came together.* I knew that I needed to do better. I knew that I could not wait until the end of the semester or year to reflect, to figure out how things went, and what I needed to change. Reflection had to be daily and changes needed to be implemented quickly." (personal communication)

Another positive result of this experience is that many of the practices that are highlighted through the self-reflection process continue to play an integral role in the classroom even after the camera disappears. It becomes easier to shift your perspective and put yourself in your students' position. When teachers think about what it feels like to be on the receiving end of their own instruction, they are better able to adapt their strategies and improve their teaching.

According to Andria Mitchell, an 8th grade language arts teacher,

> I have made reflection a greater component of my teaching practices. When I say *reflection*, I mean actually stopping and writing down what went well and what didn't at the end of each lesson. When I was recording myself and looking at the videos, I was usually surprised by the mistakes I made. I immediately wrote down suggestions about how to better prepare for the questions that my students might ask, how to ask more thought-provoking questions, where to stand when I'm talking, whether I should walk around the room or stand in one spot, or whether I should read or let the students read. I teach inclusion, standard plus, and honors students, and the successes and failures within each class vary. By intentionally establishing a time to reflect, I am able to "be better" tomorrow. (VIVA MET Idea Exchange, 2013, p. 7)

Share Your Teaching with Others

Once teachers are comfortable viewing their own teaching, they can feel empowered to share their videos with a group of trusted colleagues who can offer commentary and a fresh perspective. Ryan Kinser, an 8th grade English teacher and "teacherpreneur" with the Center for Teaching Quality (which means he teaches in the morning and spends his afternoons advancing teacher leadership in person and online, including developing Video Learning Communities, or VLCs), has taken this a step further. Kinser began a VLC at his school, which quickly spread to a dozen more schools in a semester.

"Think about a presentation, a workshop, or even a classroom lesson of your own when things just didn't click," he says. "Now can you think of a phenomenal lesson or a teacher you heard about who you just had to see in action? What would you learn about these experiences if you saw them on video? Even better, what if you had a personal learning network of folks who reflected together on each other's experiences, making adjustments, celebrating successes, and building libraries of practice?" (Kinser, 2013).

The VLC experience has transformed learning communities in Kinser's Florida district in a few concrete ways, with few start-up costs. Specifically, mentors can coach and reflect with new teachers and break down videos together. In addition, teachers with similar schedules can still observe one another's lessons, participate in valuable online chats, and benefit from specific feedback, effectively eliminating the barriers of time and space.

Finally, videos provide actionable data. "How many of your learning communities or meetings revolve around water cooler gossip or off-topic chatter or data that you just can't use?" Kinser asks. "With VLCs, you're actually looking at student behavior, teachable moments. What can we learn from this video that we couldn't learn from just talking about it?"

Of course, teachers have to set up several protocols in order to focus VLCs on productive conversations. The following are important points to keep in mind, according to Kinser:

- Participation should be voluntary, but once teachers sign up, they should commit to a specific level of engagement. At a minimum, they should add at least one video and comment on one of their colleagues' videos.
- Teachers should comment using the "glow and grow" technique, which is when teachers are asked to comment specifically on areas of strength and improvement rather than make generic comments such as "Good job!"
- Participants should coach—not evaluate—one another.
- A seven-day window for viewing and commenting on new videos should be established.
- Teachers should be encouraged to schedule a face-to-face debrief meeting date, either in a professional learning community (PLC) or at a schoolwide faculty meeting.
- Teachers should have the ability to remove their videos at any time and retain control over who views them.

Of course, it should go without saying that VLCs present challenges. Some teachers may fear technology, fear seeing themselves on camera, or worry about the security of the videos and how they'll be used. Kinser and his colleagues have addressed some of these challenges. Their VLCs are teacher-led and initiated and are never used for evaluation purposes; they're about growth and development, but trust is a prerequisite. "We are very sensitive to this fear and begin by explaining the privacy policies," Kinser explains. "These are teacher-led communities not used for punitive evaluations. It's important for any fledgling VLC to establish clear communication and policies about this" (personal communication).

To overcome teachers' concerns, the entire faculty at Kinser's school was asked to take part in a "brag session," during which they suggested outstanding lessons or strategies they knew about or had seen in action around the school. Volunteers then became "model teachers" who demonstrated these strategies on film. Kinser himself posted one of the first videos and asked for constructive criticism. "It really broke down some barriers and made people feel their expertise was valued. I wanted them to see the process in a safe space and that I was willing to be criticized in order to get better. I'd recommend having a sample video to demonstrate the power of analysis with a group."

For those without access to fancy cameras and expensive software platforms, devices such as simple digital cameras, smartphones, and tablets work just fine for recording observations. In addition, sites such as VoiceThread or a private channel on SchoolTube are perfect for sharing videos. A great starting point is TeachingChannel (www.teachingchannel.org), which has a growing community of nearly 300,000 teachers and 700 free videos that feature exemplary teaching practices—including hundreds of videos that address the Common Core State Standards. TeachingChannel also has a service called TeachingChannel Teams (www.teachingchannel.org/teams), a socially enabled, video-based private collaboration platform for schools, districts, and education organizations that lets teachers engage in deep discussions of TeachingChannel videos and upload their own videos for reflection and coaching. It's never been easier to make the transition and begin using video for self-reflection and professional development.

Ask Your Students

Besides watching their own teaching and discussing it with others, teachers can use student surveys to ask their students what they think about the classroom experience. Sarah Brown Wessling, the 2010 National Teacher of the Year and an English language arts teacher at Johnston High School in Johnston, Iowa, describes why she regularly uses student evaluations of her teaching to hone her instruction: "It's hard to do it. It's hard to put yourself out there, [but] I take them very, very seriously. It's really nice to be able to get these but they're also honest, which is exactly what I've asked of them" (Wessling, n.d.).

Wessling has been asking her students to fill out course evaluations at the end of each semester for a long time. Recently, she was inspired to redesign her course evaluations to match the seven characteristics of the Tripod Student Survey developed by Ron Ferguson at Harvard University, a version of which was used in the MET study. The characteristics are care, control, clarify, challenge, captivate, confer, and consolidate. Each of the "seven Cs" is measured using multiple survey items; the associated student perceptions can be seen in Figure 2. The data that result from a targeted survey such as this can be vital to responsive teachers who are looking to improve their teaching.

FIGURE 2: **The Seven Cs and Students' Perceptions**	
Care	My teacher seems to know if something is bothering me.
Control	My classmates behave the way the teacher wants them to.
Clarify	My teacher knows when the class understands.
Challenge	In this class, we learn to correct our mistakes.
Captivate	I like the way we learn in this class.
Confer	My teacher wants us to share our thoughts.
Consolidate	The comments I get help me know how to improve.

Wessling, like other teachers, distributes the course evaluation at the end of the semester, but she also recommends taking "temperature readings" fairly often. Asking students to report—anonymously— on what's going well, what's not going well, and where they're progressing is invaluable to improving instruction. Through these surveys, it's possible to gain insights that might otherwise be difficult, such as when and how to rethink the balance of small- and whole-group discussions in the classroom.

Teachers can learn a lot from student surveys. After all, who doesn't want to know if their students are sufficiently challenged, if their explanations are clear or confusing, or if students are comfortable asking them for help? We must remember that students perceive clear differences among their teachers and that those differences are correlated with student learning gains. Because students have an enormous stake in teaching effectiveness, student surveys need to be done carefully. With that in mind, it's best to use a validated survey and not try to construct one yourself. How often a survey is distributed is up to you. You can use it summatively at the end of a semester or school year, or you can use it several times during the year as a type of formative feedback. You can download and use the version of the Tripod Student Survey used in the MET study from www.metproject.org/resources.php. Examples and templates of other surveys are also available online.

Examine Student Work

Of course, the real proof of effective teaching is student learning. That's why the overwhelming majority of teachers agree that student growth over the course of an academic year is the most important metric in measuring their performance. According to a nationally representative survey of teachers conducted in 2010 and 2012, 85 percent of teachers say that student growth over the course of an academic year should contribute a great deal or a moderate amount to measuring their performance (Bill & Melinda Gates Foundation, 2012b, p. 32).

Controversy arises when we consider what types of student growth measures make the most sense. Teachers, understandably, value those measures closest to the class-room—those that provide the most immediate feedback for how to improve, including classroom assignments, formative assessments, and class participation (Bill & Melinda Gates Foundation, 2012b, p. 26). However, it's important that when such measures are used as part of a formal teacher development and evaluation system, they are comparable, rigorous, and reliable across classrooms and schools. It's understandable that states and districts want measures of student learning in *all* grades and subjects, so that *all* teachers are treated equally, but it's been disheartening to see some districts rush to develop nonvalidated assessments in subjects such as music and gym and then weight them in new teacher evaluation systems.

It's time to hit pause and refocus this debate. Even validated assessments in subjects such as math and literacy don't provide a complete picture of how effective a teacher has been. Measuring growth on state tests by taking into account where students start provides only one valid measure of teaching performance—but it should not account for more than half of a teacher's total evaluation score and could account for as little as one-third.

We think there's a lot of promise in common classroom assignments and student learning objectives. Nevertheless, until we know that they're high-quality, rigorous, and comparable, their best use is to provide teachers with formative and diagnostic feedback about their practice—not to make consequential personnel decisions.

There are many tools now that help teachers teach the Common Core State Standards and assess student progress. Teachers report that such tools—including the Literacy Design Collaborative and the Mathematics Design Collaborative—are incredibly powerful in raising expectations for students and enabling students to learn Common Core knowledge and skills. One key aspect of this work is that teachers often design lessons together and review the work of one another's students against a common rubric. As a teacher, you can learn more about these tools and how you might use them in your own classroom by going to www. literacydesigncollaborative.org.

Figuring out ways to ensure that teachers are in the driver's seat and able to moderate and judge one another's work against a common template and set of criteria just makes sense. That's essentially what some of the best programs— like the International Baccalaureate—do now. Teachers are usually a great source of ideas for how to maximize the impact of their teaching practice. For example, it's important to embed assessment in daily practice so students get regular and varied feedback on their work. As one teacher notes, "This cannot be accomplished without specific and tailored professional development that builds professional integrity and authentic data. Designing assessment practices with proper professional development can be a catalyst for moving school culture forward with the intent to improve practice and student outcomes." (VIVA MET Idea Exchange, 2013, p. 15)

What Districts Can Do

In addition to the lessons from the MET Project, we've learned a tremendous amount in the past four years from the experiences of districts and charter management organizations that are striving to improve student outcomes by rethinking how they develop, evaluate, promote, and retain teaching talent based on multiple measures of effectiveness.

Engage Teachers and Principals Early and Often

In support of effective teaching, school administrators should make a point to engage with educators early and often. After all, teachers and principals are the people most directly affected by new teacher support and evaluation systems. Indeed, "Teachers and administrators working together in the evaluation process will result in less stress and greater buy-in from the classroom teachers" (VIVA MET Idea Exchange, 2013, p. 13).

Schools that have had success with this strategy seek regular feedback from practitioners through built-in feedback loops such as task forces, surveys, and focus groups and make changes in response to what they hear. Districts can do this in various ways, such as by taking the following advice:

- Create working groups of teachers and principals to provide advice and ongoing information to help shape teacher feedback and evaluation systems. Pittsburgh Public Schools and the Pittsburgh Federation of Teachers formed a committee of teachers and principals to help design a teacher support and evaluation system. They worked together to identify teacher liaisons at every school to explain the new system to their colleagues and answer questions. Since then, they have formed various working groups to help implement aspects of the system, such as an annual survey of school working conditions.

- Create focus groups on various topics. The 500 teachers at the Green Dot Public Schools, a charter network in California, participated in advisory and focus groups on such topics as multiple measures, classroom observations, and student surveys in order to help shape Green Dot's plan.

- Solicit feedback through online surveys, wiki conversations, and lunchtime talks. These are strategies successfully used by Green Dot Public Schools.

- Set up online or phone hotlines to hear teachers' concerns, and answer them early and often—within 48 hours if possible. This strategy was used successfully by Hillsborough County Public Schools to build teacher understanding and support for its new system.

- Review the language used in the observation rubric your district is considering, and revise sections to specifically target your schools' needs. After reviewing a number of existing rubrics, for example, Denver Public Schools created its own to better reflect the needs of its relatively large English language learner population.

Denver's experience provides a strong example of how other districts can partner with teachers to build their professional growth systems (Jerald, 2013). Denver Public Schools and the Denver Classroom Teachers Association invited teachers to participate in design teams to help craft the district's new teacher development and evaluation system, known as LEAP (Leading Effective Academic Practice). Forty teachers and school leaders spent the spring and summer of 2010 on five design teams, which helped develop the system, and 23 separate focus groups launched the design phase of the work. The district then recruited individual schools to test the new system in the 2010–11 school year. Based on that test, LEAP's Framework for Effective Teaching was refined and simplified. After the initial pilot, more than 50 teachers led the effort to speak to other schools about their experiences, which was a critical step in getting 94 percent of the district's schools to participate in the 2011–12 LEAP pilot. Even now, 600 teacher leaders across the district meet on a monthly basis to support implementation and provide feedback.

Teachers need to be partners in developing any framework that measures effective teaching. It's a good idea for districts to create an "evaluation community" of highly qualified teachers and administrators who help create evaluations and facilitate the evaluation process.

Communicate, Communicate, Communicate

Productive and ongoing communication with educators and the public—while maintaining a positive, supportive message about the importance of great teaching—is quite possibly the most important aspect of developing and implementing an effective evaluation system.

For example, the Memphis City Schools Foundation launched its "I Teach, I Am" campaign as a way to drive community conversations around effective teaching. After the district realized that it had no programs to celebrate its most effective teachers, it decided to create one. The campaign has four primary components:

- **Peer recognition:** More than 4,000 votes (about 60 percent of the teachers) were cast in 2012 for the Prestige Award, which went to 127 of the district's highest-performing teachers.
- **Student recognition:** The Golden Apple Award goes to teachers voted most admired by students.
- **District recognition:** A paid media campaign celebrates the accomplishments of the highest-performing teachers.
- **In-school recognition:** Teacher-of-the-Month features appear in every school building.

According to Diane Terrell, Strategy Lead for the Memphis City Schools Foundation, "The most tangible impact is expressed by teachers themselves—they feel like celebrities! They are recognized and approached wherever they go: on the street, in the grocery store, at church. And it often leads to a conversation about teacher and school performance. We're told anecdotally and in surveys that it's changed teacher perceptions about the workplace. Teachers are proud to work for MCS" (KSA-Plus, 2012, p. 17).

Similarly, Pittsburgh Public Schools created its "Believe" campaign—a series of public service ads, billboards, and videos to highlight the work teachers do in their classrooms every day to increase student achievement. The campaign served to reinforce effective teaching as a key district priority and recruit teachers for new teacher leadership positions.

Virtually every school system with which the Gates Foundation has partnered notes that principals and teachers are the best messengers to talk about effective teaching initiatives. Through its teacher recognition awards, Memphis is trying to help teachers take on leadership roles and serve as key communicators to their colleagues. Denver trained nearly 1,500 teacher leaders and principals in the LEAP framework to ensure that they had a strong common understanding of what effective instruction looks like. These educators were provided with basic information—videos, a comprehensive website, newsletters, and interactive exercises—and school teams were then encouraged to customize the training tools so teacher leaders could deliver the bulk of the content to their colleagues. These are but a few examples of many that show how schools and districts are harnessing the power of effective communication and recognition to advance professional development and student learning.

Support Principals to Do the Work

As schools and districts redesign how they evaluate, develop, and recognize effective teachers, they've also come to realize that this work has huge implications for school leaders. Recent studies suggest that principals in urban districts spend only 8 to 17 percent of their time, on average, on activities related to instructional leadership. Nevertheless, other studies show that strong school leaders are essential in attracting, developing, and retaining teacher talent at the building level (Jerald, 2012).

The steps various schools and districts have taken to support their leaders fall into three main categories (Jerald, 2012):

1. Clarify the principal's role as an instructional leader by specifying the high-impact practices for which he or she will be responsible.

2. Develop principals' instructional leadership practices through job-embedded professional supports that build expertise.

3. Enable principals to succeed as instructional leaders by providing enough time and support for them to do the job well.

Many schools have recently revised or are in the process of revising their job descriptions for principals. They are requiring that principals demonstrate that they can accurately observe lessons, provide constructive feedback, and use data on teacher and student performance to plan and deliver high-quality professional development for teachers. They are also designing new evaluation systems for school leaders that align with those for teachers, thereby holding principals accountable for developing the teachers' skills and for selecting and retaining teaching talent more strategically. Adoption of the Common Core State Standards has underscored the urgency of such efforts.

This work is not limited to public school systems such as those in Memphis and Denver. Indeed, two charter management organizations—Partnership to Uplift Communities and Green Dot Public Schools (both in Los Angeles)—require principal candidates to role-play professional development sessions. Green Dot has even developed a professional development rubric to guide principals as they plan and deliver high-quality professional development, and the organization has selected expert principals to serve as Principal Professional Development Advisors whose schools serve as "lab sites" that other principals can visit.

Hillsborough County Public Schools' principal evaluation system examines how well principals retain effective teachers in their school. The district has also made a major shift in the role of its eight area directors, retitling the position "Area Leadership Director" and rewriting the job description to focus on supporting principals' instructional practices and acting as a leader of learning for principals. To support this shift, the district contracted with New Teacher Center to provide training in coaching strategies to all eight area directors over the course of a year so they could hone their questioning and feedback skills.

In addition to the strategies described above, many schools are trying to refocus their principals' meetings on instructional issues rather than on operations. An emphasis is being placed on providing one-on-one coaching and problem-solving strategies for principals; making use of walk-throughs, instructional rounds, and individual growth plans; creating professional learning communities for principals; and providing principals with assistance on data analysis and planning. Finally, a number of schools and district have committed themselves to reducing the administrative burden on principals, helping them perform tasks more efficiently, and providing them with assistance to manage day-to-day operations and protect their time for leadership practices.

Some valuable strategies that could be applied to almost any school or district include the following:

- Implement a technology platform that tracks classroom observation results, including specific areas for teacher growth. This helps principals analyze patterns in instruction, monitor teachers' progress over time, and identify professional development resources for teachers that are tied to individual needs.
- Reduce the number of meetings that require principals to be out of their buildings so they can spend more time focused on teaching and learning within their school.
- Conduct a survey in order to help identify administrative paperwork requirements that could be eliminated or

streamlined. This obviously helps principals free up more time for instructional leadership.

- Designate a new or existing staff member to be a school administration manager. This individual should be responsible for handling some of the more routine administrative functions at the school and for monitoring and protecting the principal's time to focus on instruction.
- Create a new central-office position that supports principals in recruiting, selecting, placing, and developing teaching talent. This individual would be responsible for connecting principals to the appropriate resources across the district and in the central office.

Rethink Professional Development

Even with everything we've mentioned so far, the most exciting promise of new teacher feedback and evaluation systems that are based on multiple measures is a dramatic redefinition of teachers' professional learning. New evaluation systems, new standards, and new learning technologies will require significant shifts in teaching practices. Typically, districtwide professional development systems are not designed to provide adequate support for teachers, given these new pressures. These systems need to be redesigned to personalize learning, promote higher levels of interest and engagement, support teachers' collective improvement, and effect a greater impact on teaching practices and student outcomes.

In the United States, billions of dollars are spent annually on professional development for teachers. However, most decisions about teachers' professional learning are driven by federal, state, and district policies and district purchasing decisions—not by teachers. Most professional development is highly fragmented and not linked to effective teaching systems, and it is only beginning to reflect the demands of the Common Core State Standards. In addition, research suggests that most professional development is ineffective (Darling-Hammond, 2009). Common complaints are that many professional development initiatives are limited in scope, have minimal (if any) follow-up and support, do not adequately define or measure professional development, do not incorporate constructive feedback, have little or no connection to data, and are fragmented and incoherent.

In the spring of 2013, five school districts—in Fresno and Long Beach, CA; Bridgeport and New Haven, CT; and Jefferson County, CO—took up the challenge to dramatically rethink their systems of professional development for teachers so they are more personalized, engaging, and productive. District teams met several times to learn about new, technology-enabled tools; to plan how they could best optimize existing resources, including time; and to develop a common vocabulary and set of metrics along with an improved data/technology infrastructure so they could offer and track the impact of professional development more efficiently.

Equally important, these districts are developing their new systems with the end users—teachers—in mind and involving teachers in the redesign of these systems. If teachers have a direct say in designing professional development, then it is much more likely that districts will build more effective learning systems and that teachers will have a better chance of improving their practice. The work being done in these districts is still just getting started and should be fascinating to follow. It's important to note, though, that the districts are not alone in this endeavor. Schools and districts across the country are forging ahead with similar efforts. This is both admirable and encouraging, and it should come as some relief to those school systems that are just beginning to think about making changes. Their experiences can teach us much, and we would do well to both learn from and emulate these schools at the forefront of improving teaching with multiple measures.

One of the most promising avenues is the potential to use technology and social networking to help teachers share lesson ideas, resources, and models of effective teaching:

> As the Common Core and other policies increase alignment across districts from one coast to the other, there are new opportunities to use social media to build professional peer connections for teachers. As educators, we often feel isolated from peers and constrained by our classroom activities. Social media cannot only help teachers access information more quickly but also help us evaluate its quality more rapidly. . . . [R]eflecting on your teaching and discussing it with your peers through various channels is a valuable means of professional

growth. (VIVA MET Idea Exchange, 2013, p. 22)

A Promising Future

We're excited by the progress in education we're seeing across the country. It's good news that many schools and districts are finally focused on identifying effective teaching practices and figuring out how to support teachers to be their best. The challenge now is to make sure the urgency for change is balanced with the need to ensure fair and reliable ways to develop, evaluate, and recognize teachers. It's also important that this work is done in collaboration with teachers, whose deep reservoir of expertise and knowledge will determine whether such efforts succeed.

According to research estimates, it costs between 0.4 and 0.5 percent of total district expenditures to implement the components of a teacher evaluation system that is based on multiple measures (Bill & Melinda Gates Foundation, 2013c). This translates to between 1.1 and 1.3 percent of overall teacher compensation—surely a small price to pay to better identify, support, and retain great teachers.

When you consider that better information from teacher feedback and evaluation systems should enable districts to identify their best teachers and hold onto them; provide teachers with targeted, personalized, and timely professional development; extend the reach of great teachers dramatically; and improve education outcomes for all students, we couldn't imagine a better investment.

This is a unique moment in time. Let's be thoughtful about our approach so that one day, we can say that this was the moment when we joined together to drive the long-term improvement our schools need.

To give your feedback on this publication and be entered into a drawing for a free ASCD Arias e-book, please visit **www.ascd.org/ariasfeedback**

Ensuring Effective Instruction

Use the following information to measure effective instruction, invest in improvement, and ensure high-quality data in your school and classrooms.

	Do . . .	Don't . . .
Measure Effective Instruction		
Set expectations.	• Ask your teachers to help create shared expectations for effective instruction. • Educate everyone in the system about those expectations. • Communicate expectations often, and make sure both teachers and principals understand them.	Assume that teachers and principals share a joint understanding of effective instruction or know what evidence to look for in classrooms.
Use multiple measures.	• Select measures that reflect the full set of expectations for effective instruction. • Use measures in combination: classroom observations, student surveys, and students' academic growth.	• Focus on any single measure in isolation. • Assume the need to create or custom-design observation rubrics and student surveys from scratch; start with those that already exist for a good fit.

	Do . . .	Don't . . .
	• Use a validated observation rubric that reflects teaching practices at different levels of performance. • Use measures of student learning that are rigorous, comparable, and reliable across schools and classrooms	• Rush to create new assessments that may not be comparable or of high quality just to have a measure.
Balance weights.	Consider weighting various measures equally in order to get a good picture of instruction.	Focus on any one measure too heavily, which could send the wrong signals about what's valued in good instruction.
Invest in Improvement		
Make meaningful distinctions.	Create performance categories that really identify teachers with different skill levels and influences on student learning.	Be surprised if most teachers fall within a large middle category of performance—the goal is to improve practice.

	Do . . .	Don't . . .
Prioritize support and feedback.	• Ensure that principals and other observers are skilled at giving feedback. • Tailor professional development to the individual and collective needs of teachers. • Celebrate improvement—broadcast stories of teachers who have improved their practice. • Recognize, learn from, and draw upon the strengths of teachers by sharing their practices and providing them with leadership opportunities to help others improve..	Focus solely on problems.
Use data for decisions at all levels.	• Use the information gathered to improve professional development by considering what opportunities are already offered, how they are evaluated, and whether teachers get professional development that is targeted to their needs. • Use the information to continually strengthen principals' ability to improve instruction in their buildings.	Expect teachers to improve practice on their own without providing the necessary supports.

	Do . . .	Don't . . .
Ensure High-Quality Data		
Monitor validity.	Check to see that teachers who do well on your measures produce better learning for students.	Focus teachers' time and energy on instructional practices that are not associated with student learning progress.
Ensure reliability.	• Train teachers and principals in how to perform classroom observations accurately and ensure they can identify effective instruction. • Use at least two observers, and observe more than one lesson per teacher. • Use student surveys that focus on the instructional environment in classrooms; provide a consistent process for administering student surveys and make sure results are anonymous.	Use measures that cannot be implemented consistently across observers and classrooms.
Assure accuracy.	Use a data system that accurately links students with the teachers who instruct them and verifies the time spent by each student in a teacher's class.	Hold teachers accountable for the learning of students they do not teach.

References

Bill & Melinda Gates Foundation. (2012a). *Teacher voices: Teacher advisory council yearbook 2012.* Seattle, WA: Author.

Bill & Melinda Gates Foundation. (2012b). *Primary sources 2012: America's teachers on the teaching profession, a project of Scholastic and the Bill & Melinda Gates Foundation.* Seattle, WA: Author. Retrieved from http://www.scholastic.com/primarysources/pdfs/Gates2012_full.pdf

Bill & Melinda Gates Foundation. (2013a). *Ensuring fair and reliable measures of effective teaching: Culminating findings from the MET Project's three-year study.* Seattle, WA: Author.

Bill & Melinda Gates Foundation. (2013b). *Feedback for better teaching: Nine principles for using measures of effective teaching.* Seattle, WA: Author.

Bill & Melinda Gates Foundation. (2013c). *Investing in evaluation systems that support teacher development.* Seattle, WA: Author.

Curtis, R., (2011). *Achievement first: Developing a teacher performance management system that recognizes excellence.* Washington, DC: Aspen Institute Education & Society Program.

Darling-Hammond, L. (2009). *Professional learning in the learning profession: A status report on teacher development in the U.S. and abroad.* Dallas, TX: National Staff Development Council.

Jerald, C. D. (2013). *Beyond buy-in: Partnering with practitioners to build a professional growth and accountability system for Denver's educators.* Washington, DC: Aspen Institute Education & Society Program.

Jerald, C. D. (2012). *Leading for effective teaching: How school systems can support principal success.* Seattle, WA: Bill & Melinda Gates Foundation.

KSA-Plus. (2012). *Supporting effective teaching: Communications resources for implementing new systems for teacher development and evaluation.* Seattle, WA: Bill & Melinda Gates Foundation. Retrieved from http://www.cgcs.org/cms/lib/DC00001581/Centricity/Domain/90/Effective_Teaching_Comms_Resources.pdf

Kinser, R. (2013). Blow the doors off your classroom [video]. Retrieved from www.youtube.com/watch?v=VGaPLHVmv8U

National Council on Teacher Quality. (2012). *2012 state teacher policy yearbook*. Washington, DC: Author.

VIVA MET Idea Exchange. (2013). *Reflections from the classroom: Teachers explore the Measures of Effective Teaching (MET) research experience and its influence on future education practice*. Seattle, WA: Bill & Melinda Gates Foundation. Retrieved from http://vivateachers.org/wp-content/uploads/2013/02/VIVA-MET_Final_for-web-only2.pdf

Weisberg, D., Sexton, S., Mulhern, J., & Keeling, D. (2009). *The widget effect: Our national failure to acknowledge and act on differences in teacher effectiveness*. New York: The New Teacher Project. Retrieved from http://widgeteffect.org/downloads/TheWidgetEffect.pdf

Wessling, S. B. (n.d.). Improving practice: Learning from my students [video]. Retrieved from https://www.teachingchannel.org/videos/students-improving-teaching

Related Resources

At the time of publication, the following ASCD resources were available (ASCD stock numbers appear in parentheses). For up-to-date information about ASCD resources, go to www.ascd.org. You can search the complete archives of Educational Leadership at http://www.ascd.org/el.

ASCD EDge®
Exchange ideas and connect with other educators interested in instructional leadership and multiple measures on the social networking site ASCD EDge at http://ascdedge.ascd.org.

Print Products
Building Teachers Capacity for Success: A Collaborative Approach for Coaches and School Leaders by Peter A. Hall and Alisa Simeral (#109002)

Effective Supervision: Supporting the Art and Science of Teaching by Robert Marzano, David Livingston, and Tony Frontier (#110019)

Engaging Teachers in Classroom Walkthroughs by Donald S. Kachur, Claudia Edwards, and Judith A. Stout (#113024)

Focus: Elevating the Essentials to Radically Improve Student Learning by Mike Schmoker (#110016)

The Formative Assessment Action Plan: Practical Steps to More Successful Teaching and Learning by Nancy Frey and Douglas Fisher (#111013)

Improving Student Learning One Principal at a Time by Jane E. Pollock and Sharon M. Ford (#109006)

Transformative Assessment by W. James Popham (#108018)

ASCD PD Online® Courses
Leadership for Contemporary Schools (#PD09OC07)
Leadership: Becoming a Leading School (#PD09OC43)
Leading Professional Learning: Building Capacity Through Teacher Leaders (#PD13OC010)

For more information: send e-mail to member@ascd.org; call 1-800-933-2723 or 703-578-9600, press 2; send a fax to 703-575-5400; or write to Information Services, ASCD, 1703 N. Beauregard St., Alexandria, VA 22311-1714 USA.

About the Authors

Vicki Phillips, Director of Education, College Ready, for the Bill & Melinda Gates Foundation, has committed her career to increasing educational opportunities for young people. Prior to joining the Gates Foundation, she was superintendent of Portland Public Schools (Oregon) and was secretary of education and chief state school officer for the state of Pennsylvania.

Lynn Olson is special assistant to the director of education at the Bill & Melinda Gates Foundation. She works to identify best teaching practices that can be replicated in classrooms throughout the country.